A NOTE TO PARENTS

Reading Aloud with Your Child
Research shows that reading books aloud is the single most valuable support parents can provide in helping children learn to read.
- Be a ham! The more enthusiasm you display, the more your child will enjoy the book.
- Run your finger underneath the words as you read to signal that the print carries the story.
- Leave time for examining the illustrations more closely; encourage your child to find things in the pictures.
- Invite your youngster to join in whenever there's a repeated phrase in the text.
- Link up events in the book with similar events in your child's life.
- If your child asks a question, stop and answer it. The book can be a means to learning more about your child's thoughts.

Listening to Your Child Read Aloud
The support of your attention and praise is absolutely crucial to your child's continuing efforts to learn to read.
- If your child is learning to read and asks for a word, give it immediately so that the meaning of the story is not interrupted. DO NOT ask your child to sound out the word.
- On the other hand, if your child initiates the act of sounding out, don't intervene.
- If your child is reading along and makes what is called a miscue, listen for the sense of the miscue. If the word "road" is substituted for the word "street," for instance, no meaning is lost. Don't stop the reading for a correction.
- If the miscue makes no sense (for example, "horse" for "house"), ask your child to reread the sentence because you're not sure you understand what's just been read.
- Above all else, enjoy your child's growing command of print and make sure you give lots of praise. *You are your child's first teacher — and the most important one. Praise from you is critical for further risk-taking and learning.*

— Priscilla Lynch
Ph.D, New York University
Educational Consultant

For Michael and Millie
— P.H.

Library of Congress Cataloging-in-Publication Data

Kim, Grace.
      She sells seashells : a tongue twister story / by Grace Kim ; illustrated by Patti Hammel.
          p.   cm.— (Hello reader! Level 3)
      "Cartwheel Books."
      Summary: Peter Piper and Silly Sally visit Betty Botter, reciting well-known tongue twisters along the way.
      ISBN 0-590-26584-9
      [1. Characters and characteristics in literature — Fiction.
2. Tongue twisters.] I. Hammel, Patricia, ill. II. Title.
III. Series.
PZ7.K55964Sh   1995
[E] — dc20   94-39721
                                        CIP
                                        AC

20 19 18 17 16 15 14   9/9012/0

Printed in the U.S.A.   23

First Scholastic printing, May 1995

She Sells Seashells

A Tongue Twister Story

by Grace Kim
Illustrated by Patti Hammel

Hello Reader!—Level 3

Cartwheel
·B·O·O·K·S·®
SCHOLASTIC INC.
New York   Toronto   London   Auckland   Sydney

There are funny tongue
twisters in this story.
Read the story and try to
say the tongue twisters.

This is Silly Sally.
She sells seashells
by the seashore.

Then she picks a pretty
place to picnic.

Peter Piper is there.

Peter Piper picks a peck
of pickled peppers.
A peck of pickled peppers,
Peter Piper picks.
If Peter Piper picks a peck
of pickled peppers,
which peck of pickled peppers
does Peter Piper pick?

Peter Piper picks a perfect peck.

The pair share their lunch.
Pickled peppers . . .

and great green grapes.

Peter Piper and Silly Sally go for a walk.
They see some strange sights.

Five fat frogs flying fast.

Six sick sheep.

A big black bear.

Then they see a woodchuck.

"How much wood would
a woodchuck chuck
if a woodchuck
could chuck wood?"
wonders Peter Piper.

"We shall surely see soon,"
says Silly Sally.

"Let's visit the valley and
see Betty Botter," Peter says.
So off they go.

Betty Botter is baking a cake.

Betty Botter bought a bit
of butter to put into her batter.
But the bit of butter
made the batter bitter.

So Betty bought a bit
of better butter
to put into the batter.
And the bit of better butter
made her batter better.

Betty offers something
to go with her cake.

A proper cup of coffee
from a copper coffeepot.

A loud noise comes from outside.

More sheep!

Silly Sally scolds seven silly sheep.

The seven silly sheep
shilly-shally south.

Peter Piper takes the path to the pasture.

Betty Botter says bye-bye.

Then Silly Sally goes back to the shore . . .

to sell more shells.

The end.

MG